SNEAKERS

From Start to Finish

SAMUEL G. WOODS

PHOTOGRAPHS BY
GALE ZUCKER

BLACKBIRCH PRESS, INC.
WOODBRIDGE, CONNECTICUT

Special Thanks
The publisher would like to thank Ariane Kjellquist
at New Balance Athletic Shoe, Inc. for her generous
help in putting this project together.

Published by Blackbirch Press, Inc.
260 Amity Road
Woodbridge, CT 06525

e-mail: staff@blackbirch.com
Web site: www.blackbirch.com

Printed in Singapore

10 9 8 7 6 5 4 3 2

Photo Credits: All photos © Gale Zucker, except pages 16–17,
courtesy New Balance.

Library of Congress Cataloging-in-Publication Data
Woods, Samuel G.
Sneakers from start to finish/ Samuel G. Woods : photographs by Gale
Zucker—1st ed.
    p.   cm. — (Made in the U.S.A.)
    Includes bibliographical references and index.
    Summary: Explains how sneakers are designed, cut, sewn, embroidered,
assembled, inspected, laced, and boxed for shipping.
    ISBN 1-56711-393-1
    1. Sneakers—Juvenile literature. 2. Shoe industry—Juvenile Literature.
[1. Sneakers. 2.Shoes. 3. Shoe industry.] I. Zucker, Gale, ill. II. Title.
III. Series.
TS1017.W66   1999
685'.31—dc21   99-21379
                                           CIP

CONTENTS

Americans wear sneakers everywhere. They are worn by young and old, at work and in school. And sneakers come in an amazing variety of styles, sizes, colors, and designs. Some are for running and others for basketball. There are cross-trainers and tennis sneakers. Others are for walking and still others are for hiking. Athletic shoes are so popular that they make up an $8 billion industry in the United States alone.

Just how do sneakers get designed? And how do they go from the drawing board to the shelf at your local shoe store?

A pair of nearly finished New Balance running shoes.

SNEAKER SUCCESS

New Balance Athletic Shoe, Inc. is one of the world's most successful shoe companies. In terms of sales, it is the fourth-largest athletic shoe company in the world. It is also a world leader in athletic shoe design and manufacturing.

At the factory in Lawrence, Massachusetts, New Balance workers produce an average of 3,000 pairs of shoes each day. But a great deal of work must be done before the shoes are actually cut, sewn, and assembled in the factory.

At the end of the assembly line, shoes are checked before packing. Many steps are needed before the shoes are ready to be packed.

5

THE SNEAKER CONCEPT

One of the first steps in creating a sneaker is designing it.
New Balance has a whole staff of talented people who
design and develop new products.

*Sneaker designer Ryan
Ringholz works on the coloring
for a new product.*

Above and right: *Ryan Ringholz presents a number of different design ideas for a new basketball shoe.*

The design of a sneaker combines many elements. Choices must be made on color, shape, materials, and style. To make these choices, the staff works together to consider all the possibilities. As they progress, sketches and finished drawings are done. At each stage, the staff decides on the elements that are right.

GETTING WITH THE PROGRAM

Once a design is approved, it is sent to another department. There, technicians and programmers figure out how to turn the design into a real shoe. Sometimes, special computer programs must be written to adapt a machine to a specific design. Some complicated programs must tell a machine how to sew up to 16 pieces together at one time.

Programmer Michael Vance works on his computer to create a program for one of the sewing machines.

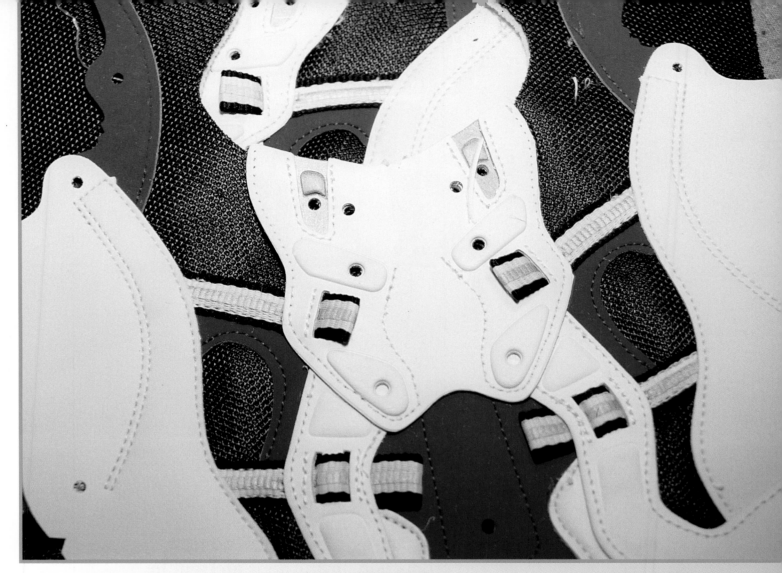

With certain models, the entire top section is sewn together at one time. A computer-programmed machine stitches all along the curves and outside edges of all these pieces.

At the beginning of production, large sheets of material are measured and cut.

STARTING LARGE

When all the planning and programming have been done, a sneaker is ready to go into production. Instructions are sent to various departments in the factory. Each department begins doing its part of the job.

In the cutting department, workers measure and cut large sheets of leather or leather-like materials (synthetics). These sheets are stapled together in groups of five or six. When they are ready, the sheets go to another department where shapes are cut from them.

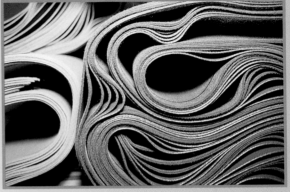

Different materials are used for different shoe models. In all cases, however, large sheets are stapled together and cut so pieces for up to 90 shoes can be cut at one time.

11

THE PIECE PROCESS

Workers cut small pieces from large sheets of material with shaped metal molds called dies (similar to cookie cutters). Each die is shaped to produce a specific part of a shoe. To make a cut, a worker first places the die on top of the material. Then a press is placed over the die. When the press is brought down, it punches the die through the material. This produces pieces in the unique shape of the die.

Top: A worker places a die in position.
Bottom: When the press comes down, it punches the die through the material.

Above top: *Dies for cutting pieces of the vamp (top of shoe) are left; dies for shoe tips are right.*
Above middle and bottom: *Cutting pieces for the side of the vamp.*
Left: *Pieces for the central part of the vamp are cut from a large sheet.* 13

A CUT ABOVE

Certain pieces are cut by a machine that is programmed by a computer. This computer-driven machine cuts large sheets of foam into pieces used in tongues (under laces) and collars (back of shoe). These foam pieces are then sewn inside pieces of fabric.

Left and above: *A computer-programmed cutting machine cuts sheets of foam used for the collar lining.*

Above left: Paper cut-outs from various dies show the many pieces that come together for the top part of a typical shoe.
Above right and below left: Pieces of the vamp are separated in bundles.
Below: Vamp pieces are all assembled on a stitching machine.

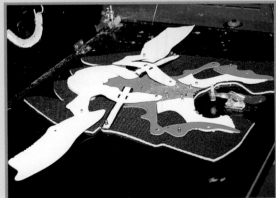

LEAVING A FOOTPRINT: THE NEW BALANCE STORY

Chairman and CEO, Jim Davis

What is today New Balance Athletic Shoe, Inc. began in 1906. Back then, the company was called The New Balance Arch Company because it made orthopedic shoes (special corrective shoes for foot problems) and arch supports.

During the 1950s and 1960s, more and more runners asked New Balance to create specialized hand-made athletic footwear. As its reputation grew, the company soon focused on custom-made running shoes.

On Boston Marathon Day in 1972, James S. Davis, a businessman and amateur runner, purchased the company. At that time, the entire operation was made up of 6 people making 30 pairs of athletic shoes per day.

The shoe they were making was called the "Trackster." It was one of the first shoes made specifically for running. And it was the first made in a wide range of widths. In 1976, the New Balance 320 running shoe was rated number one on the market by *Runner's World* magazine. This achievement gave the company worldwide recognition.

During the 1980s, New Balance grew and expanded its business significantly. By 1990, the company was approaching $100 million in U.S. sales—more than $200 million worldwide.

Today, sales are approaching $700 million worldwide, and New Balance products are sold in a total of 63 countries on 6 continents. All together, more than 1,900 people work for the company.

Large stitching machines holding nearly 100 spools of thread embroider model numbers and logos for various parts of New Balance shoes.

QUICK STITCHES

In another area of the factory, large stitching machines bob up and down rapidly. They assemble and label other parts of the sneakers. With 15 heads each, these high-speed machines can do 850 stitches per minute. They can also sew up to seven colors at the same time. These are the machines that embroider the New Balance name and model number on many shoes.

As the stitching machines work, the company name appears on what will be the back of a shoe.

Below: *Vamp pieces are each placed in position before being stitched.*
Left: *The sewn vamp comes out of the stitching machine in one piece.*

ALL SEWN UP

Once all the individual pieces of a sneaker are cut, sewn, and embroidered, they are sent to an assembling area. There, the various sections of a shoe begin to come together. Some shoes are made of more than 40 different pieces.

The top sections (uppers) of some shoes require more than a dozen pieces to be sewn together. Certain models have their tops sewn by a computer-run sewing machine. This machine must be very carefully programmed. It must stitch curves and zig-zags within a very tight area. There is little room for error.

A finished upper is trimmed and then checked before it is sent on through the production line.

21

Positioning the New Balance "N" on the vamp takes precision and skill.

THE HUMAN TOUCH

Before the tops can be finished, certain detail work must be done. The company's famous "N" must be placed on the sides of certain models. To do this, a worker positions a fabric "N" on the vamp by peeling off the back and sticking it down. Placement of this element must be exact. If it is not done correctly, the shoe will not look right. Once the "N" is in place, it is taken to another area where it is sewn.

Right: *Nearly completed uppers are ready to be attached to the inner support of a shoe (midsole).*
Below: *Final stitching for the upper often requires the skills of a worker who sews by hand.*

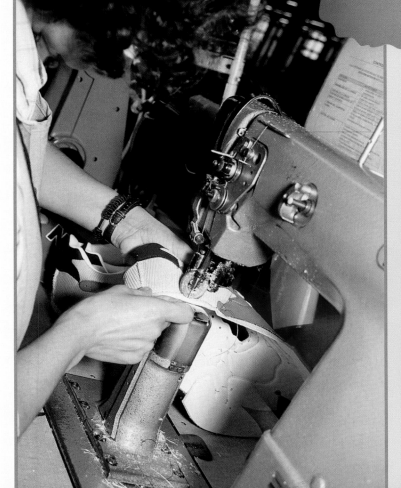

Not all stitching is done by computers. Much of the sewing can only be done by skilled human workers. Finishing the uppers of certain models, for example, requires sewing a cone-like piece. This cannot be done by a machine.

When the top pieces are all assembled, they are sent over to another area of the factory. This is where the final assembly will take place.

23

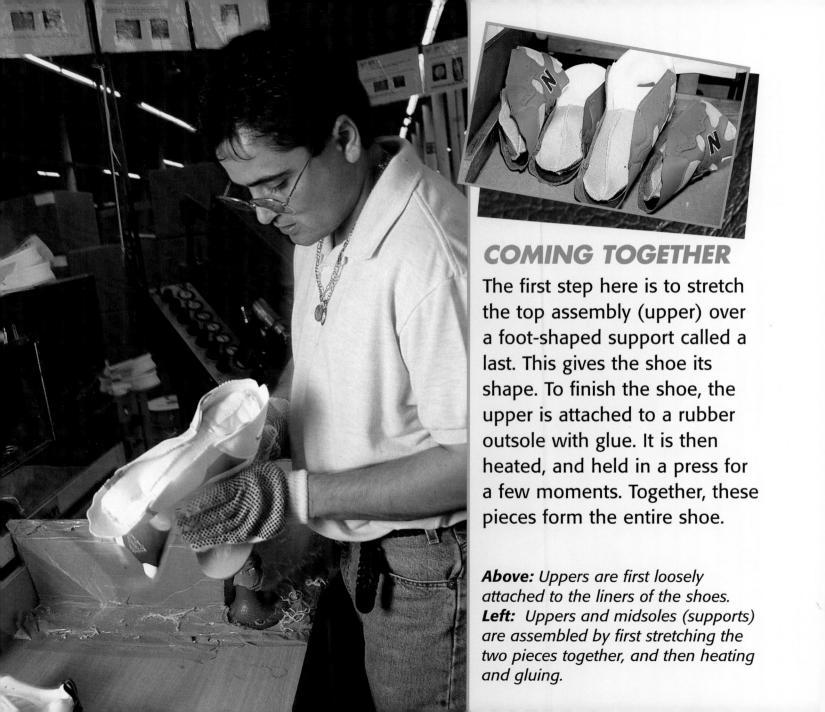

COMING TOGETHER

The first step here is to stretch the top assembly (upper) over a foot-shaped support called a last. This gives the shoe its shape. To finish the shoe, the upper is attached to a rubber outsole with glue. It is then heated, and held in a press for a few moments. Together, these pieces form the entire shoe.

Above: Uppers are first loosely attached to the liners of the shoes.
Left: Uppers and midsoles (supports) are assembled by first stretching the two pieces together, and then heating and gluing.

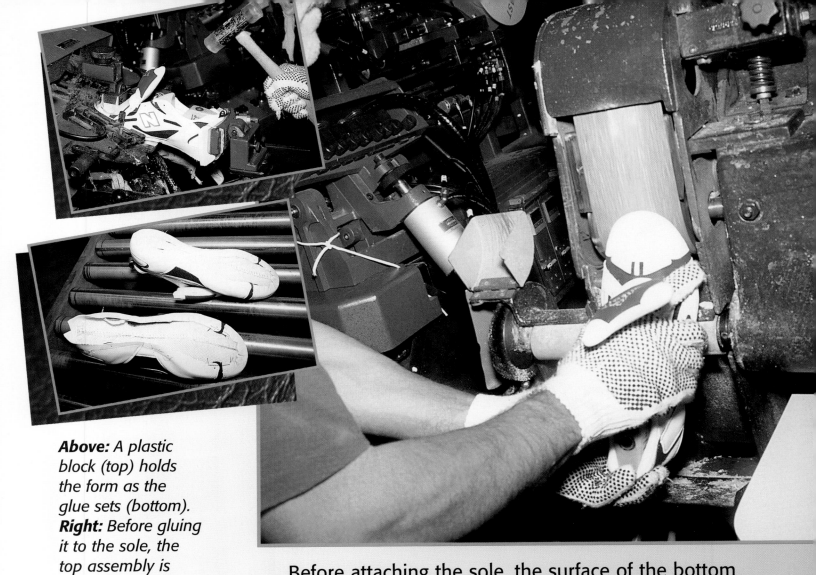

Above: A plastic block (top) holds the form as the glue sets (bottom). *Right:* Before gluing it to the sole, the top assembly is placed on a rougher, which is like a sander.

Before attaching the sole, the surface of the bottom piece is placed on a kind of sanding belt called a rougher. This roughs up the bottom and insures a better gluing surface.

YOU GOTTA HAVE SOLE

Before gluing the sole to the upper, the two pieces are fitted together. They are placed in a clamp on a revolving platform and are marked with an ultra-violet pen. The pen's markings show workers how high up the sole sits on the body. This gives them a guide for applying the glue. The ultra-violet lines don't show up in ordinary light. They can only be seen under ultra-violet light.

Above top: *Marking the upper with the ultra-violet pen.*
Above and right: *Uppers and soles are separated again (above) and heated (right) before final gluing.*

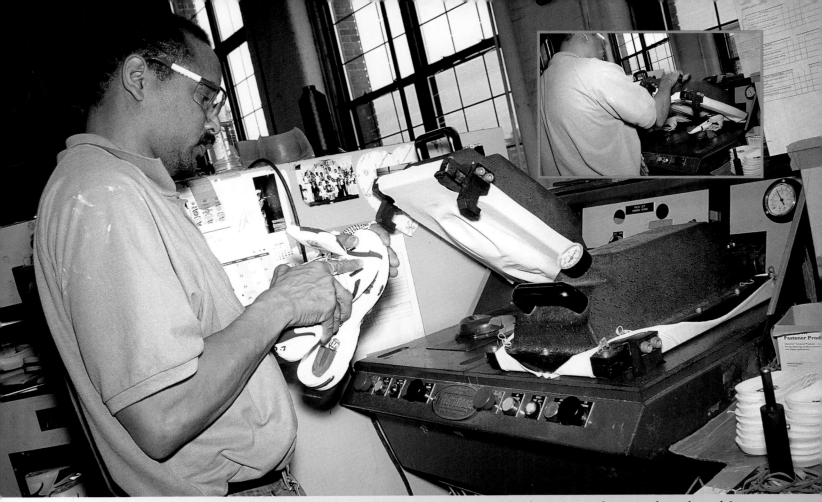

Upper and sole are fitted together before a pressure press holds them together as the glue dries.

The sole and the upper are separated and heated before the final gluing. When they are ready, the glue is applied and the pieces are re-fitted. Then they are placed under pressure in a special press. The press insures full contact between the pieces. It also allows the glue to set in exact position.

QUALITY CONTROL

Now that the shoe is nearly complete, a final inspection is done. Workers check for a tight fit and look for minor scratches, marks, or rough spots. A small polisher is used to smooth over rough areas or marks. A hot-air gun may be used to harden any glued seams. And small pieces of dirt, fabric, or thread may be blown off the shoe with an air hose.

Near the end of the production line, the shoes get a final inspection.

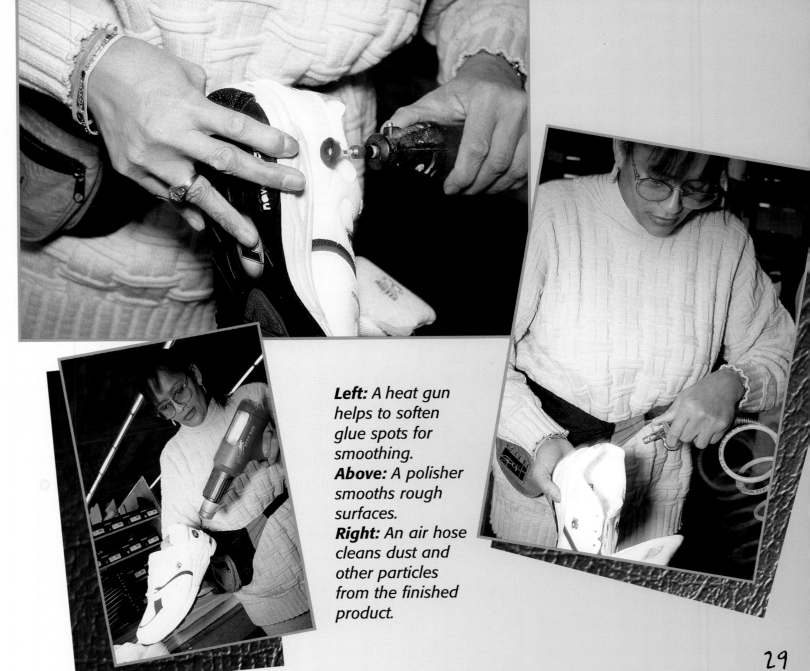

Left: *A heat gun helps to soften glue spots for smoothing.*
Above: *A polisher smooths rough surfaces.*
Right: *An air hose cleans dust and other particles from the finished product.*

29

Finished shoes are partially laced before boxing.

THE LACE RACE

Before the shoes are boxed, they are partially laced. Then they are carefully placed inside their shoebox. An identification card is also placed inside. This shows where the shoes came from and which team worked on them. It also allows proud workers a chance to take credit for a job well done!

PROUDLY ASSEMBLED IN U.S.A.

BY TEAM No. 25

new balance®

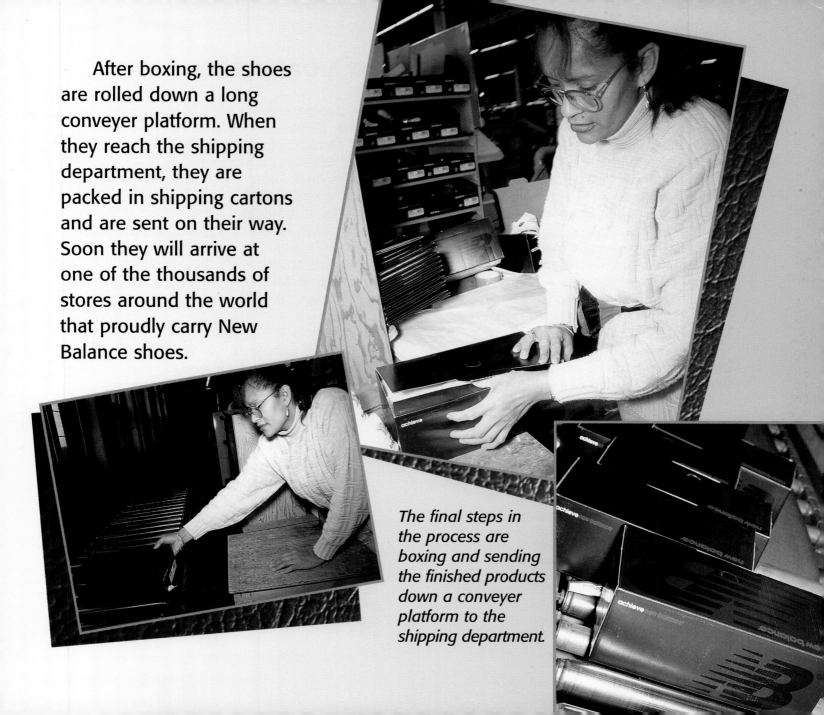

After boxing, the shoes are rolled down a long conveyer platform. When they reach the shipping department, they are packed in shipping cartons and are sent on their way. Soon they will arrive at one of the thousands of stores around the world that proudly carry New Balance shoes.

The final steps in the process are boxing and sending the finished products down a conveyer platform to the shipping department.

GLOSSARY

Adapt to make something suitable for a different purpose.

Arch support a special rise in some shoes that provides a firm surface to support the curve on the bottom of the foot.

Die a tool or device that cuts a shape or form from a material, similar to a cookie cutter.

Endorse to support or approve of something or someone.

Synthetic human-made material; not natural.

Reputation worth or character, as judged by other people.

Technician someone who works with specialized equipment.

Ultra-violet light light that cannot be seen by the human eye.

Upper top portion of a shoe.

Vamp the upper part of a shoe that covers the forepart of the foot.

FOR MORE INFORMATION

Books

Jones, George. *My First Book of How Things Are Made: Crayons, Jeans, Guitars, Peanut Butter, and More* (Cartwheel Learning Bookshelf). New York, NY: Cartwheel Books, 1995.

Kain, Kathleen. Robert Byrd (Illustrator). *All About How Things Are Made* (Inspector McQ). Chicago, IL: World Book Inc., 1995.

Lawlor, Laurie. *Where Will This Shoe Take You?: A Walk Through The History of Footwear.* New York, NY: Walker & Co. Library, 1996.

Young, Robert. *Sneakers: The Shoes We Choose!* Morristown, NJ: Dillon Press, 1991.

Web Site

New Balance Cyberpark
Stroll through this site for information on company history, exercise, and links to running and walking web sites—http://www.newbalance.com.

INDEX